We Need Fire Fighters

by Lola M. Schaefer

Consulting Editor: Gail Saunders-Smith, Ph.D.

Consultant: Robert Farmer, Fire Fighter/Paramedic, City of Upper Arlington, Ohio Fire Division

Pebble Books

an imprint of Capstone Press
Mankato, Minnesota

Pebble Books are published by Capstone Press
818 North Willow Street, Mankato, Minnesota 56001
http://www.capstone-press.com

Library of Congress Cataloging-in-Publication Data
Schaefer, Lola M., 1950–
    We need fire fighters/by Lola M. Schaefer.
    p. cm.—(Helpers in our community)
    Includes bibliographical references and index.
    Summary: Simple text and photographs describe fire fighters and their role in
our communities.
    ISBN 0-7368-0391-2
    1. Fire fighters—Juvenile literature. 2. Fire extinction—Juvenile literature.
[1. Fire fighters 2. Fire extinction 3. Occupations.] I. Title. II. Series: Schaefer, Lola M.,
1950– Helpers in our community.
TH9148.S33 2000
363.37′092′2—dc21   99-18422
                                                                                          CIP

Note to Parents and Teachers

The Helpers in Our Community series supports national social studies standards for units related to community helpers and their roles. This book describes and illustrates fire fighters and how they help people. The photographs support early readers in understanding the text. The repetition of words and phrases helps early readers learn new words. This book also introduces early readers to subject-specific vocabulary words, which are defined in the Words to Know section. Early readers may need assistance to read some words and to use the Table of Contents, Words to Know, Read More, Internet Sites, and Index/Word List sections of the book.

Table of Contents

Fire fighters put out fires.

Fire fighters spray water and foam on fires.

Fire fighters use tools
to fight fires.

Fire fighters rescue people and animals.

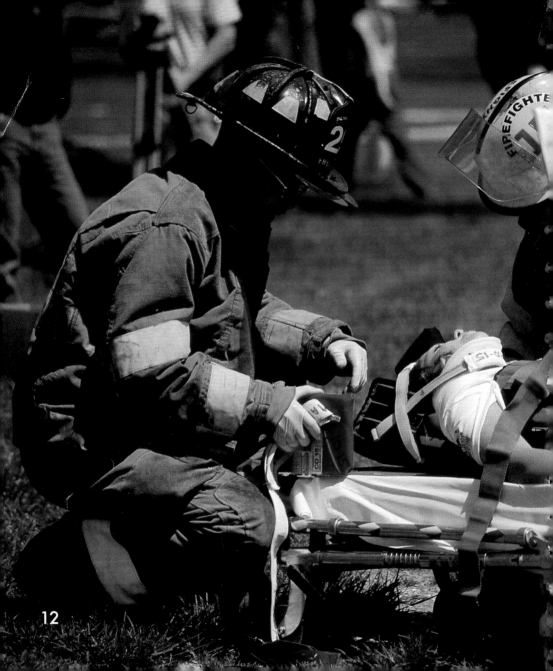

Fire fighters help people
who are hurt.

Fire fighters teach people about fire safety.

Fire fighters wear clothes
that keep them safe.

Fire fighters travel
on fire trucks.

Fire fighters keep
their equipment ready
at the fire station.

Words to Know

equipment—the machines and tools needed for a job; fire-fighting equipment includes fire trucks, hoses, and special clothing.

foam—bubbles used to fight fires

rescue—to save someone who is in danger

safe—not in danger of being hurt

spray—to scatter through the air in small drops; fire fighters use hoses to spray foam and water on fires.

tool—a piece of equipment used to do a job; fire fighters use axes to enter burning buildings when doors are locked.

Read More

Fortney, Mary T. *Fire Station Number 4: The Daily Life of Firefighters.* Minneapolis: Carolrhoda Books, 1998.

Royston, Angela. *Fire Fighters.* Eyewitness Readers. New York: DK Publishing, 1998.

Saunders-Smith, Gail. *The Fire Station.* Field Trips. Mankato, Minn.: Pebble Books, 1998.

Internet Sites

Smokey the Bear
http://www.smokeybear.com

Sparky the Fire Dog
http://www.sparky.org

USFA Kids Homepage
http://www.usfa.fema.gov/kids/index.htm

Index/Word List

Word Count: 64
Early-Intervention Level: 9

Editorial Credits
Karen L. Daas, editor; Abby Bradford, Bradfordesign, Inc., cover designer; Kimberly Danger, photo researcher

Photo Credits
David F. Clobes, 16, 20
Index Stock Imagery, 8; Index Stock Imagery/Aneal Vohra, 1
Leslie O'Shaughnessy, 4, 6
Palma Allen, 12
Photri-Microstock, 14
Steven M. Jones/FPG International LLC, cover
Unicorn Stock Photos/Jim Shippee, 18
Uniphoto, 10